Black Ghost Knifefish as Pets

Black Ghost Knifefish

A Complete Owner's Guide

Including information on purchasing and caring for
Black Ghost Knifefish and other Knifefish species as well as
feeding, breeding, health problems and more all included.

ISBN : 978-0-9923922-7-7

Printed by Lightning Source, Victoria

Disclaimer

Although the author and publisher have made every effort to ensure that the information in this book was correct at press time, the author and publisher do not assume and hereby disclaim any liability to any party for any loss, injury, damage or disruption caused by errors or omissions, whether such errors or omissions result from negligence, accident, non-functional websites, or any other cause. Any advice or strategy contained herein may not be suitable for every individual.

Foreword

In this book you will find the answers to all of your questions regarding Black Ghost Knifefish. Here you will find tips for raising, feeding and caring for your fish in addition to information about breeding, health problems and more. By the end of this book you will have the information you need to care for your Black Ghost Knifefish.

Acknowledgements

I would like to extend my sincerest thanks to my friends and family who supported me throughout this journey. I'd like to thank my wife especially for her patience with me throughout my research and writing – thank you!

Table of Contents

Chapter One: Introduction

1: Black Ghost Knifefish (Apteronotus albifrons)

When you imagine a fish, you probably envision a scaled body with paired fins floating effortlessly through the water. This image is by no means inaccurate, but it does not apply to the Black Ghost Knifefish. These fishes are extremely unique in appearance, looking more similar to an eel than to a traditional fish. In addition to their unique appearance, Ghost Knifefish are also very interesting and entertaining animals to keep as pets.

Freshwater aquarium hobbyists are always on the lookout for new and interesting species to add to their tanks. If this describes you, the Ghost Knifefish is a species you definitely want to consider. Even if you have never owned an aquarium before, reading about the Ghost Knifefish may inspire you to do so. These fish are incredibly beautiful in their own way and they are unique from other fish in that they can be tamed to the point of tolerating handling by their owners.

The Ghost Knifefish is a wonderful creature and makes an excellent addition to the freshwater aquarium. As is true with any pet, however, you should learn everything you can about these fish before you consider owning one. In order to keep your Ghost Knifefish happy and healthy you must cultivate an aquatic environment that meets the needs of your fish and, in order to achieve this, you must do some basic research. In this book you will find a wealth of information about Ghost Knifefish including basic facts about them as well as their requirements in regard to habitat and diet.

By the time you finish this book you will feel prepared to make an educated decision regarding whether these fish are the right pets for you and, if you decide that they are, you will be well on your way to knowing what you need to know to provide them with the best care you possibly can.

Useful Terms to Know

Activated Carbon – a type of carbon used in aquarium filtration; helps to remove dissolved wastes and toxins from tank water

Alkalinity – the capacity of tank water to buffer against changes in pH; a higher alkalinity means a more stable pH

Ammonia – NH3; a toxic substance that results from respiration and the breakdown of waste

Beneficial Bacteria – a term used in reference to the anaerobic bacteria that colonize a tank and serve to establish and maintain the nitrogen cycle

Biological Filtration – a natural filtration method involving the cultivation of a colony of beneficial bacteria which serve to break down wastes

Chemical Filtration – a type of filtration which utilizes chemical processes (such as activated carbon) to remove toxins and chemicals from tank water

Chlorine – a chemical often used to treat municipal water to kill bacteria; toxic to fish

Denitrification – the process by which beneficial bacteria convert nitrate in tank water into nitrogen gas to be released from the tank

Detritus – solid waste that accumulates in an aquarium

Dorsal Fin – the fin located along the top of a fish's body

Electric Organ Discharge (EOD) - a method of high frequency, tone-type (or wave-type) electricity used for communication in weakly electric fish

Filter – a piece of aquarium equipment used to remove unwanted chemicals and solid particles from tank water

Filter Media – any substance used in an aquarium filter to remove solid or organic wastes from tank water (ex: activated carbon for chemical filtration)

Gills – membranous tissues located on either side of the fish's head which absorb dissolved oxygen from water to facilitate respiration

Hospital Tank – a type of quarantine tank used to house individual fish for treatment; also used to prevent the spread of disease from one fish to the rest of the tank

Mechanical Filtration – a type of filtration designed to remove solid waste particles from tank water

Nitrate – NO3; the final product of the nitrogen cycle and a chemical toxic to fish in high concentrations (less harmful than nitrite)

Nitrite – NO2; the second product of the nitrogen cycle; highly toxic to aquarium fish

Nitrogen Cycle – the process by which beneficial bacteria break down wastes and convert toxic substances into less harmful substances (also referred to as denitrification)

pH – a measure of how acidic or alkaline water is; measured on a scale from 0 to 14 with 7 being neutral

Water Change – the process of removing and replacing a portion of tank water with fresh water; helps to reduce the concentration of heavy metals and other toxic substances

Chapter Two: Understanding Ghost Knifefish

2: Black Ghost Knifefish (Apteronotus albifrons)

The name Ghost Knifefish is given to several species of Knifefish belonging to the family Apteronotidae in the order Gymnotiformes. In order to understand Black Ghost Knifefish you must learn the basics about their evolutionary heritage and what sets them apart from other types of fish, including other types of knifefish. In this chapter you will learn not only what knifefish are, but you will also learn specifics about what makes Ghost Knifefish unique. You will also find in this chapter specific information about various species of knifefish including both the Black Ghost Knifefish and the Brown Ghost Knifefish, the two most popular species of knifefish in the aquarium trade.

1.) What Are Knifefish?

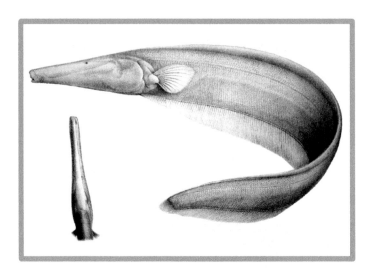

Extant species of fish are divided into three classes by body type: jawless, cartilaginous, and bony. Jawless fishes are those which descended from the first fish species, Agnathans, which evolved over 500 million years ago. These fish have small sucking mouths and typically exhibit an elongated, eel-like body shape. Cartilaginous fishes, descendant from the class Chondricthyes evolved about 280 million years ago. These fish (which include sharks and rays), are boneless, having an internal skeleton made of cartilage to provide structure and protection.

The third class of fish contains over 12,000 different species belonging to the class Osteicthyes. The largest group of fish within this class belong to the order Teleostei – fish belonging to this group are often referred to as teleost species. This third class of fish contains bony fish – fish which have true bone as well as paired fins and a variety of different body shapes depending on the type of aquatic environment they inhabit. Knifefish, the subject of this book, are a group of teleost bony fishes.

Knifefish, though related to well-known bony fishes like Cichlids and Cyprinids, have a unique body shape. These fish have long, streamlined bodies with elongated anal fins – their bodies are slender and taper toward the tail. Unlike many bony fishes, knifefish do not possess pelvic fins or dorsal fins. Rather, their elongated anal fin stretches along the underside of the body – knifefish achieve movement by keeping their bodies rigid and rippling their fin to propel themselves either backward or forward through the water.

Other morphological differences seen in knifefish (as compared to other bony fishes) is the absence of a caudal fin (tail). Some species of knifefish (namely Apteronotids) still possess a caudal fin, but it is greatly reduced in size. These fish also exhibit restricted gill openings and the anal opening is positioned either under the head or the pectoral fins (rather than under the anal fin like many species).

Knifefish also possess an electric organ which enables them to produce tiny discharges of electricity (typically only a few millivolts). Because these charges are so weak they typically do not serve to protect the fish against predators – rather, they are used to help the fish communicate and to navigate in their environment. The electric eel, which belongs to the same order as the knifefish, is the only species able to produce a strong enough electric current to stun its prey.

The order Gymnotiformes contains about 150 known species in 32 different genera. Most of the fish belonging to this group can be found in freshwater habitats in humid Neotropic regions. Knifefish are nocturnal creatures which can be found living in floodplains as well as streams and rivers. Though Ghost Knifefish are the most popular species in the aquarium hobby, other species of knifefish can be found in aquaculture. You will read more about some of these species later in this chapter.

2.) Facts About Ghost Knifefish

While there are many different species of knifefish, the name Ghost Knifefish is given to a select number of species belonging to the family Apteronotidae in the order Gymnotiformes. These fish are found primarily in the freshwater habitats of South America and Panama. What makes Ghost Knifefish different from other related species is the fact that they have a caudal fin (tail). Ghost Knifefish are also nocturnal, preferring to hunt for food at night rather than during the day.

Species belonging to the family Apteronotidae are often referred to collectively as Apteronotids. In addition to the presence of a caudal fin, several other morphological characteristics set this group of fishes apart from others in their order. Ghost Knifefish have was is referred to as a "dorsal organ" – a fleshy strip of tissue running longitudinally along the dorsal midline. These fish have very small eyes and two jaws, each lined with 1 to 2 rows of conical teeth.

Perhaps the most interesting fact about Ghost Knifefish, however, is the fact that they use electricity to communicate. This method of communication is called electric organ discharge (EOD) and it is a method of high frequency, tone-type (or wave-type) electricity. The electric organ in Apteronotid fish is made of muscle tissue and modified nerves, serving to create an electric discharge and a weak electric field around the fish. The cells that comprise this organ are called electrocytes or electroplaques and they are flat and disk-like in shape. These cells are powered by adenosine triphosphate (ATP) and work by pumping positive potassium and sodium ions out of the cell.

The two most popular species of Ghost Knifefish in the aquarium hobby are the Black Ghost Knifefish and the Brown Ghost Knifefish. Both of these species grow to be fairly large, though the Black Ghost Knifefish is the larger of the two. Both species look very similar, having a long, unscaled body with a fleshy fin on the underside of the body. As suggested by the names of the species, however, the Black Ghost Knifefish is primarily black with two white rings on the tail – the Brown Ghost Knifefish is chocolate brown in color with white piping on the dorsal fin.

Another interesting fact about Apteronotid fishes is the presence of sexual dimorphism between the sexes. With many species of fish, it is very difficult to tell the difference between male and female specimens aside from subtle differences in color. In Ghost Knifefish, however, there are clear differences between the sexes in snout size and shape. Once males of this family reach maturity, their jaws become highly elongated and some species have teeth that grow externally over their snouts. Having an elongated jaw is thought to play a role in male-on-male competition during mating among species belonging to this family of fishes.

Summary of Facts

Taxonomy: Order Gymnotiformes, Family Apteronotidae
Habitat: freshwater habitats of South America and Panama
Unique Morphology: caudal fin, dorsal organ, small eyes
Habit: nocturnal (active at night)
Diet: aggressive predator; feeds primarily on small fishes and insect larvae
Species: Black Ghost Knifefish (*Apteronotus albifrons*) and Brown Ghost Knifefish (*Apteronotus leptorhynchus*)
Size: Black - 20 inches (50 cm), Brown – 10 inches (25 cm)
Lifespan: 7 to 10 years
Communication: electric organ discharge (EOD)
Sexual Dimorphism: males have elongated jaws; some species have teeth growing externally over the snout

3.) Evolution of Ghost Knifefish

Earlier in this section you received some basic information regarding the evolutionary heritage of Ghost Knifefish. In order to truly understand this species, however, you may be interested in reading a more detailed history. As is true of all extant species of fish, the evolution of the Ghost Knifefish can be traced back to the first fishes that evolved approximately 500 million years ago. These fish, the Agnathans, were not only the first fish to evolve but also among the first vertebrates to inhabit the earth.

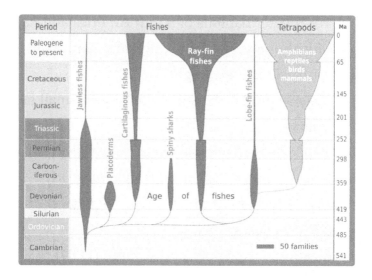

The Agnathans were jawless fish that possessed rounded mouth parts designed for filter feeding or sucking. These fish had no scales but possessed armor that protected their bodies and their internal organs. Some of the first jawed fishes to evolve were the placoderms – these fish first appeared during the Silurian period (between 443 to 419 million years ago) and dominated the Devonian period (419 to 358 million years ago). The placoderms were very large fish with armored bodies and a moveable joint between the head and body that enabled the fish to open its mouth very wide to consume prey.

Between 400 and 450 million years ago, during the same time that placoderms were prowling the earth's oceans, some of the first cartilaginous fish began to develop. Sharks, rays and skates belong to this group of fishes which have cartilage instead of bones in their bodies – it is estimated that about 900 species of cartilaginous fish are still in existence today. The largest group of extant species of fish comes from the Class Osteicthyes, or true bony fish. This class of fish first started to evolve about 410 million years ago and an estimated 12,000 species still exist today.

For millions of years, fish continued to evolve and adapt to their individual habitats. It wasn't until about 250 million years ago, however, that the superorder Ostariophysi (to which knifefish belong) came into existence. This superorder of fishes is distributed throughout the entire world (except in Antarctica) and fossils of various species have been found dating as far back as the Cretaceous period. It is believed that the common ancestor of all Ostariophysians first entered fresh water about 251 million years ago during a time when oxygen levels in the world's oceans experienced a severe decline.

Over time, the Otophysi diverged into four different groups: Cypriniformes, Characiformes, Siluriformes and Gymnotiformes. The division of these groups is thought to coincide with the breakup of Pangea, a supercontinent which existed approximately 300 million years ago and eventually broke up into the 7 continents the world knows today. Gymnotiformes are largely found in freshwater river and streams throughout the Neotropic regions of the world ranging from Guatemala to Argentina. These fishes developed electric organs and electrosensory systems which further set them apart from other related groups of fish.

Today, the Gymnotiformes group contains about 150 known species and is subdivided into the following suborder and superfamilies:

Suborder Gymnotoidei

* Family Gymnotidae (electric eel, banded knifefishes)

Suborder Sternopygoidei

Superfamily Rhamphichthyoidea

    * Family Rhamphichthydiae (sand knifefishes)

    * Family Hypopomidae (bluntnose knifefishes)

Superfamily Apteronotoidea

    * Family Sternopygidea (glass knifefishes, rat-tail knifefishes)

    * Family Apteronotidae (ghost knifefishes)

As you can see from the list above, Ghost Knifefishes belong to the Family Apteronotidae within the Superfamily Apteronotoidea in the Suborder Sternopygoidei. Most fish belonging to this family are aggressive predators which use EOD to communicate and navigate. The Black Ghost Knifefish and the Brown Ghost Knifefish both belong to the genus Apteronotus, a group of fishes that is restricted to South America.

4.) Types of Knifefish

Below you will find a brief explanation and description of some of the most popular species of knifefish, including both the Black and Brown Ghost Knifefish.

Aba Knifefish (*Gymnarchus niloticus*)

3: Aba Knifefish (Gymnarchus niloticus)

Also known as the Freshwater Rat-Tail or the Frankfish, the Aba Knifefish is one of the largest species of knifefish. This species can achieve an adult length up to 5 ½ feet (167cm) long and it can weigh as much as 40 lbs. (18.5kg). Due to its large size, the Aba Knifefish requires a minimum tank size of 300 gallons (1135 liters).

African Knifefish (Xenomystus nigri)

The African Knifefish is one of the most popular species of knifefish in the aquarium trade, largely because it is less shy than some species (like the Ghost Knifefish). This species can grow up to 12 inches (30.5cm) long in the wild though, in captivity, it tends to top out around 8 (20.3cm) inches in length.

4: African Knifefish (Xenomystus nigri)

The African Knifefish is very similar in appearance to another knifefish, the Bronze Featherback (*Notopterus*

notopterus), having a flat body with an arched back. It can be distinguished from the Bronze Featherback, however, due to its lack of a dorsal fin. The African Knifefish is uniformly gray-brown in color with a joined anal and caudal fin.

Centipede Knifefish (*Steatogenys duidae*)

The Centipede Knifefish has a very long and slender body that is ornamented with bands of brown and tan color. This particular species of knifefish has recently begun to experience more popularity in the aquarium hobby, partially due to its common name. In addition to its bands of color on the body, this species also has bars on the anal fin which give it the appearance of having myriad feet.

5: Centipede Knifefish (Steatogenys duidae)

This species of knifefish is native to South America and it can be distinguished from other species by its short, blunt snout. Compared to other knifefish, the Centipede Knifefish is fairly small, only growing up to 8.25 inches (21cm). This species is easy to care for compared to other knifefish because it is not very sensitive to changes in water parameters, though it still requires high water quality.

Glass Knifefish (*Aigenmannia virescens*)

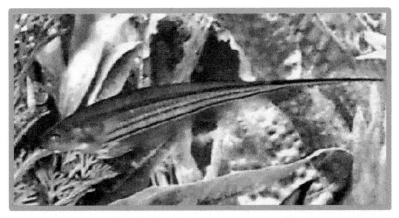

6: Glass Knifefish (Aigenmannia virescens)

What gives this species its name is the transparency of its body. The Glass Knifefish is also known for the knife-like shape of its body and for its snout being relatively short compared to other knifefish. This species is generally nonaggressive and, unlike other knifefish, tends to do well when kept in groups with others of its own species.

Clown Knifefish (Chitala ornate)

The Clown Knifefish is one of the most recognizable species of knifefish given its silver-gray coloration and the spotted pattern above the anal fin. Some specimens of the species have no spots, however, and an albino version is also possible. Generally the Clown Knifefish is similar in appearance to other knifefish, having a flat, elongated body with an arched back and long anal fin.

7: Clown Knifefish (Chitala ornate)

Because the Clown Knifefish often has difficulty acclimating to a new environment, this species is recommended for experienced aquarium hobbyists. This species can also grow to be very large, achieving an adult length around 3 ½ feet (100cm) in the wild. In captivity, however, these fish tend to reach a maximum length around 10 to 20 inches (25 to 50cm). Ideally, these fish should be housed in a tank no smaller than 200 gallons (757 liters) in capacity with plenty of open space for swimming.

Zebra Knifefish (*Gymnotus pedanopterus*)

8: Zebra Knifefish (Gymnotus pedanopterus)

This species of knifefish is particularly rare and, when it does become available in the aquarium hobby, it tends to command a high price. Having only been recognized in 1994, the Zebra Knifefish is still relatively new in the aquarium hobby. Unlike many knifefish species, however, it appears to be fairly hardy and easy to keep. What gives this species its name is its black-and-white banded patterning.

Reticulate Knifefish (*Papryocranus afer*)

9: Reticulate Knifefish (Papryocranus afer)

Also referred to as the Marbled Knifefish or the Arowana Knifefish, this species one of the more outgoing species of knifefish. Another feature which makes these fish unique is the fact that they swim differently than other knifefish. While most knifefish keep their bodies rigid and ripple their anal fin for propulsion, the Reticulate Knifefish undulates its entire body (much like an Arowana).

The Reticulate Knifefish can achieve an adult length up to 32 inches (81cm) and can weigh more than 3 lbs. (1.36kg). As suggested by the nickname Marbled Knifefish, this species has a dark body (black or brown) with light-colored mottling. The body itself has a flat, elongated shape with an arched back and a long anal fin which is joined to the caudal fin. This species also possesses a small dorsal fin.

Black Ghost Knifefish (*Apteronotus albifrons*)

10: Black Ghost Knifefish (Apteronotus albifrons)

Sometimes simply referred to as the Black Ghost, this species of knifefish is one of the most popular in the aquarium trade. Black Ghost Knifefish are named for their black coloration which is often accompanied by white banding on the caudal peduncle. This species received its name from the belief of some Amazonian tribes that the souls of the dead inhabit these fish.

The Black Ghost Knifefish can reach a length of up to 20 inches (50cm) which means that it requires a very large tank, at least 150 gallons (568 liters) in capacity. Until recently, specimens of this species available in the aquarium trade were typically wild-caught. Now, however, they are being bred commercially in Asia due to their increased popularity in the aquarium hobby.

Brown Ghost Knifefish (*Apteronus leptorhynchus*)

The Brown Ghost Knifefish is very similar in appearance to the Black Ghost though, as suggested by the name, it is dark brown rather than black in color. The Brown Ghost Knifefish also has a longer snout and only one white band near the end of its tail (compared to the two bands seen on the Black Ghost Knifefish).

Another characteristic which sets the Brown and Black Ghost Knifefish apart is their personality traits. The Brown Ghost Knifefish tends to prefer to remain on the bottom of the tank, only coming out to feed. For this reason, it is recommended that they not be kept with very boisterous or curious tank mates that could cause the fish stress. Compared to the Black Ghost, Brown Ghost Knifefish are also somewhat smaller, achieving a maximum length around 10 inches (25cm).

Chapter Three: What to Know Before You Buy

11: Black Ghost Knifefish (Apteronotus albifrons)

Before you bring home any new pet, there are certain preparations that need to be made. First, you need to know whether there are any legal restrictions or requirements for keeping such a pet and you need to know whether you can keep it with any other pets you already have. You should also take the time to think about the details of owning your new pet – how much will it cost and what are the advantages of this pet over another? In this chapter you will learn the answers to these questions and more to help you decide whether the Ghost Knifefish is the right choice for you and your family.

1.) Do You Need a License?

Before you bring home a new pet of any kind, it is wise to make sure that there are no legal restrictions in your area for doing so. Certain species are regarded as threatened or endangered which may limit your ability to obtain them as well as your legal right to own them. Luckily, there are few restrictions regarding the keeping of aquarium fish. For more information regarding legal issues for keeping aquarium fish in your area, keep reading.

a.) Licensing in the U.S.

In the United States, aquarium hobbyists are not required to obtain a license or permit to keep aquarium fish. You are only likely to encounter problems if you plan to harvest fish from a local body of water (including the ocean). Because Black Ghost Knifefish are not native to the United States, however, you should not require a permit to purchase, keep or breed these fish. Some states require aquarium fish suppliers to obtain a license for species of fish that are gathered from or can survive in native waters of the state, but since Ghost Knifefish are a tropical species, these rules are unlikely to apply.

b.) Licensing in the U.K.

As is true in the U.S., you are not required to obtain a permit to purchase, keep or breed Ghost Knifefish in the United Kingdom. Generally, permits and licenses are only required for individuals gathering fish from native waters (which does not apply to the Ghost Knifefish). If you plan to import fish into the country, however, you may be required to obtain authorization from the Fish Health Inspectorate (FHI). This will also be required if you plan to open an aquaculture production business.

2.) How Many Should You Buy?

Before you consider how many Ghost Knifefish you should buy you need to think about how many you can safely accommodate. While these fish are often sold as juveniles measuring no more than 2 inches (5 cm) long, they can grow upwards of 12 inches (30.5 cm) long at maturity. The most important factor to consider in deciding how many to buy, then, is how many you have space for. The general rule of fishkeeping is to have no more than 1 inch (2.5cm) of fish per gallon of tank capacity. In using this rule, you must consider the adult length of the fish (up to 18 inches or 45 cm) rather than its size when you purchase it.

You also need to think about the fact that Ghost Knifefish are semi-aggressive and a territorial species. Generally, it is recommended that you keep these fish singly or in groups of 6 in a very large tank. It is not recommended that you keep Ghost Knifefish in pairs, especially if both of the fish are males.

3.) Can Ghost Knifefish Be Kept with Other Pets?

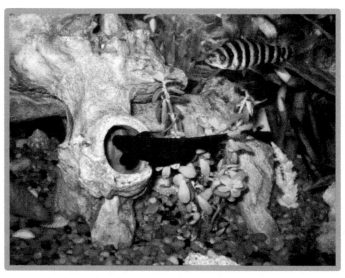

12: Black Ghost Knifefish (Apteronotus albifrons)

When it comes to keeping aquarium fish, many hobbyists prefer to keep what is known as a "community tank" – a tank which houses multiple different species of fish. In order to cultivate a community tank successfully, however, you must choose species of fish that are going to get along. It is important to remember that Ghost Knifefish are not only a large species, but also a predatory one – they are likely to feed on any small fish in your tank so do not house them with any fish smaller than 6 inches (15 cm) long.

Another thing you need to remember is that Ghost Knifefish can be fairly aggressive and territorial. If you plan to keep your Ghost Knifefish with other species, make sure the tank is very large so each fish has adequate space. Do not keep your Ghost Knifefish with other aggressive species or any that are likely to nip at the fish's fins (such as tetras). Some of the best species to keep Ghost Knifefish with include Discus Fish, Angelfish and other peaceful South American cichlids. Do not keep Ghost Knifefish with other species of electric tropical fish.

4.) Ease and Cost of Care

It is important to realize that Ghost Knifefish are not a species recommended for the beginner. These fish are fairly difficult to care for so they are only recommended for experienced aquarium hobbyists. In addition to assessing your level of expertise in the field, you should also consider whether you can afford to keep a Ghost Knifefish before you go out and buy one. In this section you will receive an overview and estimate of both the initial costs and monthly costs associated with keeping Ghost Knifefish so you can determine whether or not you can appropriately care for one of these beautiful fish.

a.) Initial Costs

The initial costs associated with keeping Ghost Knifefish are those which you must cover in order to prepare for and purchase your fish. These costs may include the cost of the fish itself as well as the cost of the aquarium, equipment and other necessary supplies. Below you will find an explanation of each of these costs as well as an estimate per fish and per pair of fish (remember, if you keep more than one Ghost Knifefish it should not be in groups containing fewer than 6 specimens).

Purchase Price – though Ghost Knifefish are becoming more popular in the aquarium hobby, you may not be able to find them at your local fish store. Generally, your best bet is to find and order these fish online directly from a breeder or from an aquarium supply company. You can expect to pay between $15 and $25 (£9.75 - £16.25).

Aquarium – given that Ghost Knifefish are a fairly large species, you will need a large aquarium (at least 150 gallons/568 liters) to accommodate them. If you already have a large tank established, you may not need to make any additional purchases. For those who are starting a new tank, however, you should plan to spend at least $800 (£520) on a 150-gallon (568 liter) tank or more on a larger one.

Basic Equipment – in addition to the tank itself, you also need to purchase several pieces of equipment to establish and maintain your Ghost Knifefish tank. The type and quality of equipment you purchase will affect the price but you should be prepared to spend between $200 and $500

(£130 - £325) on equipment such as filtration, heating and lighting for your tank.

Other Supplies – some of the other supplies you will need to get your Ghost Knifefish tank started may include a bottle of dechlorination solution, filter media, light bulbs and aquarium decorations. The cost for these items will vary depending on your tank size and setup but you should be prepared to spend between $50 and $150 (£32.50 - £97.50) on additional supplies.

Initial Cost Chart		
Cost	**One Fish**	**Two Fish**
Purchase Price	$15 to $25 (£9.75 - £16.25)	$30 to $50 (£19.50 - £32.50)
Aquarium	$800 (£520)	$1,000 (£650)
Equipment	$200 to $500 (£130 - £325)	$200 to $500 (£130 - £325)
Other Supplies	$50 to $150 (£32.50 - £97.50)	$50 to $150 (£32.50 - £97.50)
Total	$1065 to $1475 (£692 - £959)	$1,280 to $1,700 (£832 - £1105)

b.) Monthly Costs

The monthly costs associated with keeping Ghost Knifefish are those which you must cover in order to properly care for your fish. These costs may include the cost of fish food, water treatments, medications and equipment repairs/replacements. Below you will find an explanation of each of these costs as well as an estimate.

Fish Food – the Ghost Knifefish is a predatory animal which means that you will need to feed it live, meaty foods rather than traditional flake foods. The cost for these foods will vary depending on the size of your fish and the number you have but you should plan to spend $20 (£13) per month or more on food.

Water Treatment – in order to keep your Ghost Knifefish tank clean and its water clear, you will need to perform routine water changes (generally on a weekly basis). Before you add any new water to the tank, you must treat it with a dechlorination solution to remove the chlorine. In order to keep a supply of this water treatment solution on hand, you shouldn't need to spend more than $10 (£6.50) per month.

Medications – the only time you will need medications for your Ghost Knifefish is if they become sick. As long as you provide a healthy diet and proper care for your fish, this shouldn't happen often. Just to be safe, however, you may want to budget an average of $5 (£3.25) per month to cover the cost of medications.

Equipment Repair/Replacement – you may not need to make monthly repairs or replacements to your aquarium equipment, but it is always wise to be prepared in the event of an emergency. In addition to the cost of repairs, you should also budget for the replacement of filter media as well as replacement bulbs for your lighting system. You will not need to purchase these items each and every month, but your yearly cost may be around $100 (£65) which, averaged over 12 months, is about $8 (£5) per month.

Monthly Cost Chart		
Cost	One Fish	Two Fish
Fish Food	$20 (£13)	$40 (£26)
Water Treatment	$10 (£6.50)	$10 (£6.50)
Medications	$5 (£3.25)	$5 (£3.25)
Other	$8 (£5)	$8 (£5)
Total	$43 (£28)	$63 (£41)

5.) Pros and Cons of Ghost Knifefish

In addition to considering the costs of keeping Ghost Knifefish, you should also think about the pros and cons of doing so. These fish are incredibly beautiful and unique from other species, but they are not suited to every tank or every aquarium hobbyist. Below you will find a list of the pros and cons associated with keeping Ghost Knifefish as pets so you can decide whether or not they are a good option for you and your tank.

Pros for Ghost Knifefish

- Incredibly beautiful and unique in appearance
- May develop interesting behaviors – can be tamed and may even permit handling
- Generally does well in a freshwater South American biotope tank
- Can be kept with other peaceful species with similar habitat requirements
- Becoming more popular in the pet industry, thus making it more readily available

Cons for Ghost Knifefish

- Grows very large and thus requires a lot of space
- Should not be kept in groups smaller than 6
- May prey on smaller species of fish (might not do well in all community tanks)
- Very sensitive to fluctuations in water parameters
- Requires very high levels of oxygen – should only be kept in a fully-established tank
- Should not be kept with other species of electric fish
- Predatorial and semi-aggressive by nature (particularly within its own species)

Chapter Four: Purchasing Ghost Knifefish

13: Black Ghost Knifefish (Apteronotus albifrons)

After reading the basics about Black Ghost Knifefish and other Knifefish species, you should have a good idea whether or not this is the right pet for you. If you have decided that a Ghost Knifefish is indeed a good choice, you may be ready to learn more about how and where to purchase them. In this chapter you will learn the basics about where to find Ghost Knifefish and how to select a healthy specimen.

1.) *Where to Buy Ghost Knifefish*

Depending where you live, you may not be able to just stop in to your local pet store and find Ghost Knifefish. These fish are increasing in popularity within the aquarium trade but they cannot yet be said to be "common". In this section you will learn some of the best places to find Ghost Knifefish in both the U.S and U.K.

a.) Buying in the U.S.

You may be able to find Ghost Knifefish for sale in some of the larger U.S. pet supply stores like PetCo and PetsMart. If you live in a small town, however, this may not be the case. An alternative to looking for these fish in stores is to purchase them online directly from a breeder or from an aquarium supply website. Below you will find a list of some places to find Ghost Knifefish online.

Some recommended websites for purchasing Ghost Knifefish include:

LiveAquaria.com.

http://www.liveaquaria.com/product/prod_display.cfm?c=7
47+870+857&pcatid=857

PetSolutions.com.

<http://www.petsolutions.com/C/Live-Freshwater-Fish-
Knifefish/I/Black-Ghost.aspx>

AquaticstoYourDoor.com.

<http://www.aquaticstoyourdoor.co.uk/Black-Ghost-Knife-
Fish.html>

b.) Buying in the U.K.

Purchasing Ghost Knifefish in the U.K. is very similar to
buying in the U.S. – you may be able to find them at your
local pet store, but you should not necessarily count on it.
Your best bet may be to purchase these fish online. If you
do purchase fish online, make sure the company has safe
and ethical shipping practices so your fish are not exposed
to any extreme temperatures or long shipping times.

Some online sources for purchasing Ghost Knifefish
include:

Tropical Fish by Post.

<http://www.tropicalfishbypost.co.uk/black-ghost-knifefish.html>

LiveAquatics.co.uk.

<http://www.liveaquatics.co.uk/shop/knifefish/black-ghost-knife/367>

LiveFish.com.au.

<https://www.livefish.com.au/tropicals/miscellaneous/black-ghost-knife-fish-15cm.html>

2.) *How to Select a Healthy Ghost Knifefish*

After doing all the research to determine whether a Ghost Knifefish is truly the right pet for you, the last thing you want to do is bring one home just to lose it a few days or weeks later. Many inexperienced aquarium hobbyists make the mistake of buying their fish without taking the time to make sure they are healthy. If you bring home a fish that is already sick, there may be little you can do to keep it alive – it may also infect the other fish in your tank.

Here are some tips for selecting healthy fish from your local pet store:

- Look around the store before you even look at the fish – if it is dirty and ill-kept, do not purchase there
- Speak to the professionals working at the store – they should be at least somewhat knowledgeable about the animals they are caring for and selling
- Look at the tanks themselves – if they are not clean or if there are a large number of dead fish in the tanks, do not buy from that store
- Observe the fish you are thinking about buying to see if they exhibit healthy movement – they shouldn't be lethargic or swimming erratically

- If you can, watch the fish being fed to see if they have a healthy appetite – if the fish doesn't eat, it may be sick
- Check the fish's eyes, gills and fins – there shouldn't be any visible signs of discharge or discoloration
- Make sure there are no bumps, cuts or growths on the body and fins of the fish

If, after performing these basic checks, you are able to determine that the fish is healthy you can think about purchasing it. Bringing home a healthy fish doesn't stop with the pet store, however – you also need to perform some basic precautions when you get the fish home. Before you add your fish to an established tank you should keep it in quarantine for at least two weeks. During this time, observe the fish for signs of illness – even if the fish appears healthy when you buy it, it could still be a carrier of disease. If, after two weeks, your fish still appears healthy you can go through the process of acclimating it to your tank.

Chapter Five: Caring for Ghost Knifefish

14: Black Ghost Knifefish (Apteronotus albifrons)

The Ghost Knifefish makes a wonderful pet, but it may not be the right choice for everyone. These fish can be very sensitive to changes in water parameters and they need a significant amount of space. This being the case, you should make sure that you are able to provide for the needs of a Ghost Knifefish before you bring one home. In this chapter you will learn the basics about the habitat requirements for this species as well as what type of tank and other equipment you will need. You will also learn about the nutritional needs of Ghost Knifefish so you can provide yours with a healthy diet.

1.) *Habitat Requirements*

The Ghost Knifefish is native to the warm waters of South America, primarily the Amazon River. In order to ensure that your fish thrive in your home aquarium, you should seek to match your home tank to the parameters of the Ghost Knifefish's natural environment as much as possible. The key water parameters you should seek to achieve are as follows:

pH Level: 6.5 to 6.7 (slightly acidic)
Water Hardness: 80 to 150 ppm (slightly soft)
Temperature: 72° to 76°F (22° to 24°C)

In addition to the basic parameters mentioned above, there are other conditions you should seek to replicate. In its native habitat, for example, the Ghost Knifefish is used to fast-flowing water. To recreate this in your home aquarium, you may need to invest in a high-powered filtration system that will provide adequate water flow for a large tank. You will read more about recommended tank equipment in the next section of this chapter.

Aside from the chemical aspects of creating an ideal habitat for your Ghost Knifefish, you also need to think about the physical components of your tank. Because this species can grow up to 20 inches (51 cm) long, you need to provide them with plenty of space. Ideally, a Ghost Knifefish should be kept in a tank no smaller than 150 gallons (568 liters) in capacity, though larger is always better. If you plan to keep your Ghost Knifefish with other fish in a community tank, you would be wise to invest in a larger aquarium.

If you hope to create a natural décor scheme in your Ghost Knifefish tank, you might consider using sand or fine pebbles as substrate – this is the type of substrate found in this species' native habitat. Ghost Knifefish are a nocturnal species and tend to be very shy during the day. This being the case, you should plan to provide your fish with plenty of hiding places such as large rock caves and tall plants.

These fish also prefer dim or subdued lighting, so adding some floating plants to the surface of the tank water will also be beneficial.

a.) Maintaining Water Parameters

Now that you understand the basics of Ghost Knifefish habitat requirements, you may be wondering how much work is involved in maintaining that environment. For the most part, a successful freshwater aquarium does not require much maintenance. Once your tank has cycled and a colony of beneficial bacteria has been established, your tank chemistry should remain fairly stable on its own (as long as you do not overfeed your fish or overstock the tank). There are certain basic things you must do, however, to keep your tank running properly.

The most important aspect of tank maintenance is performing routine water changes. As mentioned earlier in this book, a water change is simply the process of removing and replacing a portion of tank water with fresh water. You should plan to replace 15% to 20% of your tank's volume on a weekly basis along with one larger water change around 25% of the tank volume once per month. When you refill the tank, make sure to use water that is the same temperature as the tank and treat it with dechlorinating solution beforehand to remove chlorine and other heavy metals that could harm your fish.

Though performing a water change is a simple enough task, there is a proper way to go about it. To get the most out of your water changes you should invest in an aquarium gravel vacuum. A gravel vacuum is simply a hollow plastic tube connecting to a length of tubing which can be used to siphon water from the tank. The benefit of using this device is that it enables you to dig deep into the substrate to siphon out accumulated wastes such as uneaten fish food and feces that, if left to accumulate further, could have a negative impact on the water quality in your tank. When using a gravel vacuum, make sure to clean out the areas around and underneath your tank decorations.

In addition to performing weekly water changes, you will also need to replace your filter media once every three to four weeks. The type of filter media you use will depend largely on the type of filter you choose – you will read more about your options in the next section of this chapter. Chemical filter media like activated carbon should be entirely replaced once a month while some mechanical filter media like sponges can sometimes be rinsed out and reused. If your filter has a biological filtration component like a BioWheel, do not clean or replace it, otherwise you run the risk of destroying your tank's colony of beneficial bacteria which could cause the tank to re-cycle.

b.) Cycling Your Tank

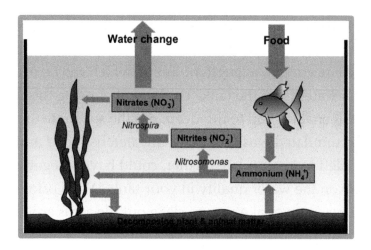

Throughout this book you have seen the terms "nitrogen cycle" and "denitrification" several times. The nitrogen cycle is simply the process through which beneficial bacteria convert the harmful substances that result from the breakdown of waste (namely ammonia and nitrite) into less harmful substances like nitrate. Once these substances are converted into nitrate, it can be removed from the tank via routine water changes.

In order for the nitrogen cycle to become established in your tank, you must first cultivate a colony of beneficial bacteria. For the most part, you can simply set up your tank and allow it to run for two weeks or so, "seeding" it occasionally with fish food to encourage the growth and reproduction of beneficial bacteria. A faster (and perhaps more reliable) method, however, is to add live beneficial bacteria directly to the tank. You can find products like this online or at your local pet store.

Establishing a colony of beneficial bacteria and cycling your tank is absolutely necessary before you add your Ghost Knifefish to your tank. These fish do not possess scales which makes them very prone to stress due to changes in water parameters. Cycling the tank will create a more stable environment and a safer environment in which to keep your fish. Do not run the risk of losing your Ghost Knifefish by adding them to your tank before it has cycled.

2.) *Setting Up the Tank*

Knowing the tank requirements for a Ghost Knifefish is only half the battle – you must also be able to cultivate and maintain those requirements within your home tank. As it has been mentioned, Ghost Knifefish are a very sensitive species which makes them somewhat difficult to keep. If you make sure that your tank is fully established and cycled before you add your fish, however, they are much more likely to thrive. In this section you will learn the basics of how to choose and set up a tank for your Ghost Knifefish.

a.) Choosing a Tank/Location

You already know that Ghost Knifefish can grow to be very large so they require a large tank. What you may not realize is that there are several different options when it comes to choosing a tank. Aquariums can be made from a variety of different materials but two of the most common are acrylic and glass. Glass is typically clearer and does not distort viewing angles in the way that acrylic can, but it is also at least twice as heavy – when you are considering a 150-gallon tank, that is a big difference.

Another factor to consider in thinking about a glass vs. an acrylic tank is durability. Acrylic tends to scratch fairly easily but, as long as the scratches are not too deep they can be buffed out. Glass is more likely than acrylic to crack or break, so an acrylic tank may give you some added peace of mind. In the end, however, it is ultimately a matter of preference which option you choose.

In addition to the materials from which your tank is made, you also need to think about its shape. A standard aquarium comes in a rectangular size but other shapes are available – you can find bow-front tanks that provide a unique viewing experience or even square or triangular tanks to make use of corner space. Just be sure that, in choosing the type of tank you want, you consider the needs of your fish as well as your own personal preference – the tank must provide adequate swimming space above all else.

Once you have chosen your tank you need to think about where you will place it. Again, a 150-gallon tank is going to be incredibly heavy once it is full of water so you are unlikely to move it once you fill it up. Choose a location that will give you an easy and pleasurable view of the tank but do not place it in a location where it will be in danger of being bumped or knocked over by heavy foot traffic. You also need to think about the fact that Ghost Knifefish are fairly timid fish so you shouldn't put the tank in a place where it is going to be noisy all the time.

Additional considerations in regard to tank location include ease of access and sunlight. That unused niche in your home may seem like the perfect spot to fill with an aquarium, but will you be able to access it easily for maintenance? You should be able to access all sides of your tank for easy cleaning. In regard to sunlight, do not place your tank in an area that receives direct sunlight because it will cause excess algae growth and will also make it more difficult for you to maintain a stable tank temperature.

b.) Selecting the Right Equipment

In order to cultivate and maintain a thriving aquatic environment within your home, you need to install certain pieces of equipment in your Ghost Knifefish tank. The key pieces of equipment you will need include: filtration, heating and lighting. Below you will find an explanation of these systems as well as some options for the type of equipment you might need

Filtration

This is one of the most important aspects of maintaining a healthy Ghost Knifefish tank – the quality of your tank water depends on the quality of your filtration system. When it comes to choosing a tank filter, you may many different options. Not all of these options are well-suited to a Ghost Knifefish tank, however. Ideally, you should look for a high-powered filtration system that can accommodate a very large tank and provide moderate to fast water flow. Keep in mind that, depending on the size of your tank, you may need more than one filter to accomplish this.

The most common types of filters used in large tanks such as those designed for Ghost Knifefish are:

Power Filter – a power filter is probably the most popular type of filter in the aquarium hobby in general because it is inexpensive and easy to use. These filters come in a variety of sizes so you can easily find one (or more than one) to accommodate your Ghost Knifefish tank. Power filters are a type of external filter that hangs on the back of the tank – they possess a tube that siphons water up out of the tank, passing it over various forms of filter media before trickling it back into the tank at the surface.

One of the main benefits of power filters over other options is that they are very easy to install – all you have to do is set up the filter and plug it in. Power filters may also come with adjustable flow rates so you can create the ideal level of circulation in your Ghost Knifefish tank. Another benefit of these devices is that they typically offer three-stage filtration (mechanical, chemical and biological) which will help to keep the water quality in your tank high.

Canister Filter – a canister filter is one of the most popular types of filter for large tanks because it can accommodate a great deal of filter media. Canister filters are a type of external filter which means that they do not hang on the back of the tank, nor must they be submerged in the tank water. Rather, a canister filter can be hidden below the tank in a storage cabinet with inlet and outlet tubes running behind the tank.

Most canister filters are designed with multiple media baskets to hold different types of filter media. The benefit of this is, of course, that you can customize your filter to provide whatever type of filtration your particular tank needs. Filter media for canister filters comes in a variety of forms to provide chemical, mechanical and biological filtration to keep your tank clean. Compared to a power filter, a canister filter does take a little more effort to install and to maintain, but it provides greater filtering power.

Wet/Dry Filter – this type of filter is typically recommended for saltwater tanks, but it can also be beneficial for very large freshwater tanks. A wet/dry filter is most well-known for providing excellent biological filtration. This is particularly important for a Ghost Knifefish tank because these fish are very susceptible to changes in water chemistry – a tank that has efficient biological filtration in place is more likely to be stable in terms of water parameters.

The reason these filters have their name is because the biological filter media is exposed to both air and water. This allows for the most efficient colonization of beneficial bacteria in the tank. The downside of wet/dry filters is that they can be challenging to install and they may require the use of additional tanks or containers for use as a sump or overflow box. If maintaining biological filtration in your tank is a key concern, however, a wet/dry filter is one option you should definitely consider.

Heating

As you already know, the Ghost Knifefish is native to the Amazon in South America – this means that it is used to a warm-water environment. Ideally, you should maintain your Ghost Knifefish tank at a temperature between 72° and 76°F (22° to 24°C). In order to accomplish this, you will need to equip your tank with some type of heating system. The most popular types of tank heaters are listed below:

Hang-on Heater – a hang-on heater is perhaps the most basic (and also the most popular) type of aquarium heater. Like hang-on filters, these heaters are partially submerged in the tank and attached to the tank wall with suction cups to keep it from falling into the tank completely. Hang-on heaters come in a variety of different sizes to accommodate small and large tanks but, for a very large tank, you may need to purchase two.

The challenge with hang-on heaters is that they do not always provide even heat distribution. The vertical orientation of the heater itself typically results in the water around the heater being the correct temperature while areas at the extremes of the tank may be cooler. If you plan to use hang-on heaters in your Ghost Knifefish tank, consider buying two and space them evenly throughout the tank to ensure proper heat distribution.

Submersible Heater – a submersible heater is, as the name suggests, one that can be submerged directly in the tank. As opposed to hang-on heaters, this type of heater is typically installed horizontally near the bottom of the tank. This ensures that the heat is distributed evenly across the length of the tank and that the water near the bottom of the tank isn't cooler than the rest. These heaters come in a variety of sizes to accommodate small and large tanks, so you shouldn't have a problem finding one adequate for your Ghost Knifefish tank.

Inline Heater – if you are looking for a high-quality and reliable method for heating your Ghost Knifefish tank, you cannot do much better than an inline heater. Inline heaters are typically connected to the return line of your aquarium filter so that the water is warmed as it is returned to the tank. These filters are compact and operate externally, which means that you do not lose any internal tank space. Most inline heaters allow you to adjust the tank temperature to a certain range or even a specific degree, making it incredibly effective. These heaters are usually more expensive than your basic hang-on heater, but they provide even and stable heating for your tank.

Lighting

As you already know, Ghost Knifefish are nocturnal creatures so the lighting needs for your tank may differ from that of a traditional community tank. The lighting in a Ghost Knifefish tank should be dim and subdued – you may even want to look into lighting systems that imitate nocturnal lighting (sometimes referred to as lunar lighting). Below you will find a list of basic options for aquarium lighting:

Standard Fluorescent – standard fluorescent lighting systems are still one of the most common options in aquarium lighting. These bulbs are easy to find and fit into most standard fixtures, coming in a range of wattages between 15 and 40. One benefit of standard fluorescent lighting is that the bulbs come in a wide range of colors on all sides of the spectrum – they are also energy efficient and run cool, negating the need for an auxiliary fan.

Compact Fluorescent – compact fluorescent lighting systems are similar to standard fluorescent systems except for the fact that the bulbs are smaller and more energy efficient. One thing you need to be wary of with compact fluorescents, however, is that high-wattage bulbs may produce heat that could impact the water temperature in your tank if you aren't careful.

LED – light emitting diode (LED) lights are one of the newest innovations in aquarium lighting and they are quickly becoming one of the most popular. These lights are incredibly energy efficient and long-lasting while still producing light as bright as any other bulb. One of the unique benefits of LED lighting is that they can be used to simulate nocturnal lighting conditions which is particular useful in a Ghost Knifefish tank.

*NOTE: High-powered lighting systems such as VHO and metal halide are not necessary for a Ghost Knifefish tank because these fish do not require bright or intense lighting. In fact, lighting that is too bright my cause your Ghost Knifefish to remain in hiding.

3.) *Feeding Ghost Knifefish*

The key to keeping any pet healthy is to provide it with a high-quality and nutritious diet. Before you can plan a diet for your Ghost Knifefish, however, you need to understand the basics of their nutritional needs. What do these fish eat in the wild and what will they eat in captivity? You will find the answers to these questions and more in the following pages of this section.

a.) Nutritional Needs

The Ghost Knifefish is a predatory and carnivorous species which means that a majority of its diet comes from meat-based sources. In the wild, these fish tend to feed on aquatic insect larvae and small fish, though they may also eat some crustaceans or other invertebrates that come their way. In captivity, Ghost Knifefish tend to accept live foods eagerly, but some may require time to get used to frozen or pellet foods. It all depends on the individual fish.

Until recently, many specimens of Ghost Knifefish sold for the aquarium trade were wild-caught. Wild-caught specimens of fish are notorious for being picky eaters, unlikely to accept anything other than the foods they would find in their native habitat. Today, however, Ghost Knifefish are becoming more popular and are being captive-bred in large numbers in Asia. Captive-bred specimens of the species will still prefer live foods, but they will be more likely to accept other foods than wild-caught specimens.

b.) Types of Food

As it has been mentioned, Ghost Knifefish subsist on a diet of small fish and insect larvae – they may also eat small crustaceans and other invertebrates. Some of the best foods to feed Ghost Knifefish include:

Brine shrimp	Tubifex worms
Daphnia	Feeder fish
Chopped earthworms	Chopped prawns
Bloodworms	Carnivore pellets

Some Ghost Knifefish have also been known to accept certain vegetables like peas, though these food should not form the majority of the fish's diet. In addition to live foods, Ghost Knifefish may also accept frozen forms of the worms and other insects listed above. Some Ghost Knifefish will even learn to accept flake foods as long as they are formulated for carnivorous species.

c.) How Much to Feed

Feeding Ghost Knifefish can be tricky since they are a nocturnal species and notorious for being shy. Some owners of these fish recommend feeding them twice a day in order to encourage them to come out of hiding more often, though feeding once per day is adequate as well. In regard to the amount you feed your Ghost Knifefish, there is no exact amount recommended – it depends on the size and age of your fish as well as its activity level.

A general rule of thumb for feeding fish is to offer small amounts at a time – no more than can be consumed within a 5-minute period of time. If you feed your Ghost Knifefish at the same time each day, it may eventually get used to you and could even begin to accept food directly from your hand. This is a charming characteristic that is unique to the Ghost Knifefish.

Chapter Six: Breeding Ghost Knifefish

15: Black Ghost Knifefish (Apteronotus albifrons)

Breeding aquarium fish can be both exciting and challenging. If you are successful, you get to experience the wonders of nature in seeing your fish reproduce and raising the babies to adulthood. It is not always easy to breed fish, however, depending on the species and on the ease with which they breed in captivity. Unfortunately, reports of successful breedings for Ghost Knifefish are few but this shouldn't stop you from trying it for yourself. If you are interested in breeding your Ghost Knifefish, the information in this chapter will help you to learn how.

1.) *Basic Breeding Info*

When it comes to breeding, aquarium fish can be divided into two main categories: egg layers and livebearers. Livebearers are those species which give birth to live, fully developed young – examples include mollies, swordtails, guppies and platies. Egg layers, on the other hand, lay eggs which hatch several days after being released and fertilized (a process called spawning). Ghost Knifefish are an egg-laying species of fish.

Within the category of egg-laying fish there are several further distinctions. Some species deposit their eggs on rocks or broad-leafed plants while others dig a hole or nest in the substrate in which to deposit them. Ghost Knifefish are egg-scatterers which means that they disperse their eggs over a wide area rather than depositing them in a single location. Once the eggs are laid, they generally take between 4 and 7 days to hatch.

In order to get your Ghost Knifefish to breed successfully in captivity, you must simulate the conditions under which they would breed in their native environment. Ghost Knifefish are native to the warm, fast-flowing waters of South America so they are most likely to breed in a large tank of warm water with a good flow. You should also make an effort to match the tank parameters to the water parameters that Ghost Knifefish prefer.

The parameters for a breeding tank are as follows:

Tank Size: 100 gallon minimum (378 liter)
Substrate: marbles or smooth pebbles
Water: treated with dechlorination solution
Temperature: about 82°F (28°C)
pH Level: about 6.7
Filtration: chemical, mechanical and biological
Water Flow: moderate flow
Decorations: tall plants and floating plants
Lighting: dim and subdued
Conditioning: earthworms, bloodworms, brine shrimp and prawns

2.) The Breeding Process

Using the information provided in the previous section, set up the breeding tank for your Ghost Knifefish. Once the tank has been established to the required parameters you can introduce your adult fish – one male and three females. As noted earlier in this book, you should be able to discern between male and female Ghost Knifefish once they reach sexual maturity. In adulthood, males of the species have a more horse-like face and females of the species may be thicker in the body. Females may also have smaller eyes that are white in color while a male's eyes are slightly larger and dark.

After introducing the fish to the breeding tank, you will need to condition them on a high-quality diet to prepare them for spawning. This diet should include protein-rich, meaty foods like chopped earthworms, bloodworms, adult brine shrimp and chopped prawns. As you condition the fish, observe their behavior for signs of mating and spawning. Over time, you may notice that the male pairs off with one of the female fish – once this happens, you may want to remove the other females from the tank.

Because Ghost Knifefish are nocturnal, they are most likely to spawn at night. This being the case, you should check your tank every morning for eggs. The eggs will be very small and are likely to fall into the gaps between the marbles or pebbles in your tank – this is a good thing because the adults will eat their eggs if they can reach them. Once your fish have spawned you should be careful not to disturb the eggs until they hatch – if you expose them to air or otherwise change the conditions in the tank they may grow fungus and die.

3.) Raising the Babies

Once your Ghost Knifefish have spawned, you should consider removing the adults from the tank. Like many fish, knifefish do not tend to care for their young – in fact, they are likely to eat their own eggs. If the eggs have been properly fertilized, they should hatch within 4 to 7 days. For the first few days after hatching, the fry (baby fish) will subsist on the remainder of their yolk sac so they will not require a lot of food. After they absorb their yolk sacs, however, you should begin to feed the fry small amounts of food several times a day.

The ideal food for baby Ghost Knifefish is infusoria. Infusoria are tiny microscopic organisms which live in freshwater ponds. To prevent contaminating the tank water in your breeding tank, do not attempt to gather your own infusoria unless you are sure the source is safe and clean. Rather, look for a commercial culture online or at your local pet store. As the fry grow, you will be able to feed them crushed protein pellets and bloodworms.

It is important to note that Ghost Knifefish fry have a very high mortality rate – it is not uncommon for only 10 out of 100 eggs to hatch at all. Do not be disappointed if your first spawning yields similar results – simply adjust your process and try again using the knowledge you gained from the last attempt. Some Ghost Knifefish may prefer a different pH or temperature than others, so pay attention to what your particular fish like and make notes of absolutely everything during the breeding process.

Chapter Seven: Keeping Your Ghost Knifefish Healthy

16: Black Ghost Knifefish (Apteronotus albifrons)

As is true for any pet, there is only so much you can do to keep your Ghost Knifefish healthy. Providing them with a clean environment and a nutritious diet will definitely help, but your fish are likely to be exposed to disease at some point during their lives. The key to ensuring a swift and full recovery is to learn everything you can about the health problems your fish may face so that you can identify and treat them as quickly as possible. In this chapter you will learn the basics about what types of diseases are common in Ghost Knifefish and how to treat them. You will also receive some tips for preventing illness.

1.) Common Health Problems

The Ghost Knifefish is a species of freshwater tropical fish which means that it is prone to developing the same diseases as other freshwater species. You should be aware that these fish have no scales and are thus more prone to becoming stressed or ill due to changes in the water parameters in their tank (see ammonia poisoning). Aside from these dangers, however, you should also be familiar with the symptoms of various freshwater fish diseases so you can quickly identify any illness in your Ghost Knifefish and start treatment immediately.

<u>Some of the most common diseases seen in this species are:</u>

Ammonia Poisoning	Ich (White Spot)
Chilodonella	Mouth Fungus
Costia	Septicemia
Dropsy	Trichodina
Finrot	Velvet

a.) Common Freshwater Fish Diseases

Ammonia Poisoning

This particular condition is incredibly dangerous for aquarium fish but it is also easily preventable. Ideally, the ammonia level in your tank should be 0 ppm – if the level in your tank approaches even 1ppm, your fish may start to exhibit signs of ammonia poisoning. You can easily measure the ammonia level in your tank using an aquarium water test kit from your local pet store (some pet stores may even test a sample of your tank water for free).

The most common signs of ammonia poisoning in fish include inflamed gills, gasping for air at the surface, loss of appetite and red streaks on the body. Because Ghost Knifefish are timid fish that tend to hide during the day, if your fish starts coming out often and hangs out near the surface of the tank, it is most likely a sign that something is wrong and you need to start treatment immediately.

The first thing you should do to treat ammonia poisoning is to perform a significant water change – about 25% to 50% of the tank volume. You may also want to check the pH in your tank and make sure it is below 7.0 – ammonia becomes even more toxic to fish at high pH levels. In addition to these things, you may want to reduce the amount you feed your fish (especially if you are overfeeding) for a few days to give the beneficial bacteria in your tank time to catch up to the biological load of your tank.

Chilodonella

This disease is caused by a protozoan parasite called *Chilodonella cyprinii* and it is seen in freshwater fish all over the world. Chilodonella is often brought about by poor water quality which creates an environment that is ideal for the parasite to reproduce – fish that are stressed by poor water quality already are more likely to succumb to infection by the parasite.

Some of the most common symptoms of Chilodonella include labored breathing, lethargy, rubbing against tank objects and clamped fins. Physical signs may include excess mucus production and a cloudy film over parts of the body. The longer the infection goes untreated, the worse the symptoms will get and the less likely a full recovery becomes. Young fish are particularly at risk for death due to severe infection.

As long as the infection is diagnosed early and treatment is started quickly, many fish stand a good chance of recovery from Chilodonella. Unlike some parasites, Chilodonella is not affected by heat so you do not need to increase the temperature in your tank. Use of Acriflavine drugs has been shown to be effective as have salt baths. You will read more about how to perform a salt bath in the Common Freshwater Fish Treatments section.

Costia

This disease is a parasite infection caused by the parasite *Ichthyobodo necatrix* (formerly known as *Costia necatrix*, hence the name of the disease). Costia is an invasive disease in which the parasite attaches itself to the skin of its host and burrows into the epidermal cells, feeding on the fish itself. Once attached, the parasite multiplies rapidly which results in an infestation which can quickly become dangerous for the host fish.

Some of the most common symptoms of this condition include loss of appetite, labored breathing, clamped fins and redness or inflammation of the skin and gills. As the infection progresses, you may also see a blue-gray slime coating on the body of the fish. In extreme cases for which treatment is not provided, fin disintegration is also likely to occur. If the gills are severely affected, it is also possible for the fish to asphyxiate.

The most effective treatment for this condition is a bath in potassium permanganate solution or sodium chloride solution. Other medications which may be effective include Malachite green, Methylene blue and Formalin.

Dropsy

This condition, also referred to as "Malawi bloat" for its propensity to affect Malawi Cichlids, is not a disease in itself but a symptom of a bacterial infection. Dropsy manifests in the form of severe bloat which may impact the ability of the fish to remain submerged. Fish suffering from this condition may also have raised scales and a lessening of body coloration.

The first step in treating this condition should be to improve water quality by performing a 25% water change every other day. If the fish's condition does not improve within a few days, treatment with a salt bath or antibacterial medications.

Finrot

This condition is fairly common in aquarium fish, particularly in those which have sustained fin damage due to nipping by other fish. Because Ghost Knifefish have a long, fleshy anal fin it is particularly prone to nipping by certain species of fish (particularly tetras). Finrot is typically caused by bacteria, namely *Aeromonas hydrophila* and *Aeromonas liquefaciens* – these bacteria are opportunistic which means that they may be present in the tank but won't necessarily cause an infection until the fish has already been weakened by stress or injury.

One of the first signs of finrot is the appearance of red streaks on the fins of the fish. As the infection progresses, the edges of the fins may become frayed and will start to deteriorate. Over time, the fins may become so severely damaged that they are reduced to stumps. Antibiotic medications are the most common treatment for this condition but it can be difficult to find the right one because finrot may be caused by a variety of different bacteria. Some of the best medications to try include erythromycin, minocycline and sulfadimidine.

Ich (White Spot)

This is one of the most common diseases affecting freshwater fish and it is caused by a protozoan parasite called *Ichthyophthirius multifiliis*. Like many parasites, Ich tends to appear when water quality in the tank declines and when fish become more susceptible to infection due to stress. This disease presents as small white spots on the skin and fins of fish – these spots are similar in size to grains of salt. As the spots spread, they cause irritation to the fish, making them scratch against tank objects.

Other symptoms associated with Ich may include lethargy, loss of appetite, labored breathing and clamped fins. This disease is incredibly contagious so it is generally not helpful to remove a single fish from the tank for treatment – rather, you should treat the entire tank. One of the most effective ways to treat an Ich infection is to speed up the life cycle of the parasite by slowly increasing the tank temperature to 82°F (28°C) over a period of several days. Treatment with medications may also be effective.

Mouth Fungus

This particular condition is a bacterial infection caused by gram-negative bacteria called *Flavobacterium columnare* – for this reason, mouth fungus is sometimes referred to as Columnaris. Like most bacteria, the bacteria responsible for mouth fungus may be present in the tank without causing any harm until the water quality declines and the fish become stressed. Once the infection sets it, it may result in symptoms such as fluffy growths on the mouth which may progress to sores and lesions along the head.

Perhaps the most effective treatment for mouth fungus is an antibacterial medication like phenoxyethanol or nifurpirinol. Treatment with salt baths or tea-tree oil has also been shown to be effective in treating this condition. The best treatment, however, is prevention – this condition can easily be prevented by keeping your water quality in your tank high.

Septicemia

Also called viral hemorrhagic septicemia (VHS), septicemia is a highly fatal infection disease that affects both freshwater and marine fish. This disease is caused by a virus belonging to the order *Mononegavirales* and it can be transmitted through tank water or contaminated food. Common symptoms of this disease include red streaks on the fins and body as well as hemorrhaging around the eyes. Infected fish may also become lethargic and lose any interest in food.

The virus responsible for septicemia tends to present in times when the water quality in the tank declines. Thus, improving water quality is the first necessary step in treatment for this disease. Treatment with medications or medicated fish foods may also be effective. Some recommended medications for septicemia include Kanacyn or Tetracycline.

Trichodina

Also referred to as "aquarium slime disease," trichodina is caused by protozoan parasites belonging to the genus Trichodina. Fish that are infected with this parasite may exhibit a grayish film on the skin as well as white bumps or lesions about the size of the head of a pin. Other symptoms may include gasping at the surface, scraping against tank objects and loss of appetite.

Trichodina parasites can multiply quickly in the tank and they are capable of surviving for up to 24 hours without a host body. Because the disease is so contagious, if one fish begins to present symptoms it is likely that the others in the tank have already been infected so you should treat the whole tank rather than the singular fish. Common treatments for this condition include Paraform, Formalin and Malachite green.

Velvet

This particular condition is often confused with Ich because it presents in a similar manner. A velvet infection results in the appearance of small yellow or gray spots, almost like dust, covering the body of fish. This condition results from a parasitic infection by parasites belonging to the genus *Oodinium*. For this reason, Velvet is sometimes referred to as Oodiniasis.

In addition to the dust-like coating infected fish exhibit, some other common symptoms of Velvet may include difficulty breathing, flashing, rapid gill movement, lethargy, loss of appetite and clamped fins. There are many treatments available for this disease including copper- and quinine-based medications. Extreme caution is recommended in using these medications with Ghost Knifefish, however, since they are very sensitive due to their lack of scales. Acridine and Acriflavine are generally deemed to be safer medications for this species.

b.) Identifying Infections in Fish

In addition to these specific conditions, your Ghost Knifefish may be exposed to other infections at some point in their lives. The medication you use to treat the disease will depend on the type of infection it is – bacterial, fungal or parasitic. Below you will find a list of symptoms associated with each type of infection:

Bacterial Infection – lethargy, loss of color, fraying fins, cloudy eyes, bloated body, open sores or abscesses, red steaks, inflammation, bulging eyes, difficulty breathing

Fungal Infection – erratic swimming, scratching on tank objects (flashing), darting, cotton-like tufts on skin or mouth

Parasite Infection – inactivity, loss of appetite, visible spots or worms, rapid breathing, scratching on tank objects, white film on body, excess mucus

c.) Common Freshwater Fish Treatments

Treatment methods vary depending on the disease for which you are treating. Below you will find a list of some of the most common treatments used in the aquarium hobby as well as a brief description regarding what diseases they may be effective against.

Acriflavine – this medication is a wide-spectrum remedy, effective in treating both fungal and bacterial infections as well as some protozoan diseases. When used as a bath, a 1% concentration used at a dosage of 10ml/450 liters is typically recommended.

Copper Sulfate – this chemical can be very toxic to fish (especially sensitive species like Ghost Knifefish) so you should use it with extreme caution. In addition to treating some external parasites, copper sulfate can also be used to control pest snails in the freshwater tank.

Formalin – this medication is particularly useful in the treatment of external parasites and egg fungus. When using formalin as a treatment, be aware that it can reduce the amount of oxygen in the water so you should increase aeration when using this medication.

Hydrogen Peroxide – though not commonly used as a treatment for disease, hydrogen peroxide can be useful in adding oxygen to water very quickly. This may come in handy if one of your fish jumps out of the tank or if your tank equipment malfunctions and you need to increase the oxygen content in your tank before your fish become hypoxic. Dosage for hydrogen peroxide is recommended at 1mg of a 3% solution per 4.5 liters of water.

Malachite Green – this medication is widely regarded as one of the most effective treatments for fungal infections in fish, though it may also be effective against certain parasites. For a long term bath, use a concentration of 0.1mg/liter and, for a 30-second dip, use a concentration of 50mg/liter.

Methylene Blue – this mediation is commonly available, so you should have no trouble finding it in the aquarium aisle at your local pet store. Methylene blue is used to treat parasite and fungal infections, particularly Ich (white spot). When using this medication, make sure to remove activated carbon from your filter because it will interfere with the efficacy of the treatment.

Potassium Permanganate – this medication has a reputation for being toxic when not used properly, so it is not as common as it once was. When used properly, however, it can be effective as a treatment against parasites and for use in sterilizing aquarium equipment. To use this medication in treatment for parasites, create a 2mg/liter concentration as a bath for the infected fish.

Saltwater Bath – a saltwater bath involves adding aquarium salt to the tank water for a limited period of time. This type of treatment is effective against bacterial and fungal infections, though it has also been known to treat parasite infections in some cases. When using a salt bath, make sure to do so in a separate container – do not add the salt directly to your tank. You should also remember that Ghost Knifefish do not have scales so you may need to be careful when creating a saltwater solution – no more than 0.1% to 0.3% concentration is recommended.

2.) *Preventing Illness*

You have probably heard the saying that the best treatment for any disease is prevention and it is definitely true when it comes to keeping your Ghost Knifefish healthy. These fish are particularly sensitive to changes in water parameters so, once they fall ill, it can be difficult to achieve a full recovery. You already know that keeping your water quality high and providing your fish with a nutritious diet will help to prevent disease, but some other aspects of disease prevention which you may need to know include setting up a hospital tank and acclimating fish slowly.

a.) Setting up a Hospital Tank

A hospital tank is simply a separate tank designed to be used in quarantining sick or injured fish. Ideally, your hospital tank should be set up following the same parameters as your main tank, thus reducing the risk that your fish will suffer any stress or shock during the transfer. Having a hospital tank setup enables you to isolate and treat a sick or injured fish without exposing the rest of the tank to potentially toxic medications.

In setting up a hospital tank there are a few things you should consider:

- Keep the bottom of the tank bare to make clean-up easier on yourself
- Consider using a sponge filter to provide gentle filtration that won't interfere with medications
- Have a hospital tank setup all the time just in case you need it
- Decorate the tank sparsely but provide your fish with places to hide

b.) Acclimating Fish Slowly

When adding fish to your tank it is imperative that you make the transition slowly – any sudden changes in tank temperature or water chemistry can be very dangerous for your fish. If you are adding new fish to an established tank, make sure you quarantine them for at least two weeks first (this is where your hospital tank comes in handy) to ensure that they are healthy.

When it comes time to acclimate your new fish, place them in a plastic bag filled with water from the hospital tank.

Next, place the entire bag in the new tank, floating it on the surface for at least 30 minutes to allow the water in the tank to acclimate to the temperature in your tank. After 30 minutes, add a small amount of water from the tank to the bag and continue making small additions every 10 minutes or so until the bag is full. Once the bag is full, carefully net your fish and release them into the tank – do not dump the entire bag into the tank for fear of changing the water chemistry in your tank.

Chapter Eight: Ghost Knifefish Care Sheet

17: Black Ghost Knifefish (Apteronotus albifrons)

In reading this book, you will find a vast wealth of information about the Ghost Knifefish and other knifefish species. As you prepare to purchase and setup your own tank, you may find that you have questions regarding specific information you read. Rather than flipping through the entire book for the answer to your question, consult the quick-reference care sheet in the following pages.

1.) Basic Information

Taxonomy: Order Gymnotiformes, Family Apteronotidae
Habitat: freshwater habitats of South America and Panama
Unique Morphology: caudal fin, dorsal organ, small eyes
Habit: nocturnal
Diet: aggressive predator; feeds primarily on small fishes and insect larvae

Species: Black Ghost Knifefish (*Apteronotus albifrons*) and Brown Ghost Knifefish (*Apteronotus leptorhynchus*)

Size: Black - 20 inches (50 cm), Brown – 10 inches (25 cm)

Communication: electric organ discharge (EOD)

Sexual Dimorphism: males have elongated jaws; some species have teeth growing externally over the snout

2.) Tank Requirements/Set-Up

Water Type: freshwater
Habitat: Amazon, South American
pH Level: 6.5 to 6.7 (slightly acidic)
Water Hardness: 80 to 150 ppm (slightly soft)
Temperature: 72° to 76°F (22° to 24°C)
Circulation: moderate to fast flow

Tank Size: minimum 150 gallons (568 liters)

Tank Material: glass or acrylic

Maintenance: weekly/monthly water changes, vacuuming gravel, replacing filter media monthly

Lighting: dim or subdued

Decorations: sand or gravel substrate, plants and driftwood

Filtration: three-stage filtration recommended; power filter, canister filter or wet/dry filter

Heating: hang-on, submersible or inline filter recommended

Lighting: standard fluorescent, compact fluorescent or lunar LED recommended

3.) Nutritional Needs/Feeding

Diet: carnivore

Type of Food: live or frozen; some may accept flake foods

Options: brine shrimp, daphnia, earthworms, bloodworms, tubifex worms, feeder fish, prawns, pellets

Frequency: once or twice per day

Amount: as much as can be eaten in 5 minutes

4.) Breeding Tips

Breeding Type: egg layer (egg scatterer)

Hatching: after 4 to 7 days

Tank Size: 100 gallon minimum (378 liter)

Substrate: marbles or smooth pebbles

Water: treated with dechlorination solution

Temperature: about 82°F (28°C)

pH Level: about 6.7

Filtration: chemical, mechanical and biological

Water Flow: moderate flow

Decorations: tall plants and floating plants

Lighting: dim and subdued

Conditioning: earthworms, bloodworms, brine shrimp and prawns

Fry Mortality Rate: about 10 out of 100 survive

Feeding Fry: infusoria to start, progress to ground protein pellets and bloodworms

Chapter Ten: Relevant Websites

Throughout this book you have received valuable information regarding the care and keeping of Ghost Knifefish. There is a great deal of information out there about these fish, so you should not assume that reading this book will make you an expert. If you truly want to provide your fish with the best care possible, you should endeavor to learn everything you can. In this chapter you will find a collection of relevant websites and resources for further information about Ghost Knifefish in these categories:

Feeding Ghost Knifefish

Caring for Ghost Knifefish

Health Information for Ghost Knifefish

General Information about Ghost Knifefish

1.) Food for Ghost Knifefish

The key to keeping your Ghost Knifefish healthy is to provide him with a healthy diet. In this section you will find a number of resources regarding information on designing and providing a healthy diet for your fish.

United States Websites:

"Black Ghost Knife Fish." Aquarium Advice. <http://www.aquariumadvice.com/forums/f29/black-ghost-knife-fish-profile-by-aidan-261639.html>

"Feeding Habits in Fish." Aquatic Community. <http://www.aquaticcommunity.com/fishfood/feedinghabits.php>

"Knifefish." Petco.com. <http://www.petco.com/caresheets/fish/Knifefish.pdf>

"Carnivore Foods." Drs. Foster and Smith. <http://www.drsfostersmith.com/fish-supplies/aquarium-fish-food/carnivore-aquarium-fish-foods/ps/c/3578/7927/7933>

United Kingdom Websites:

"Predators: The Knifefishes." Practical Fishkeeping.
<http://www.practicalfishkeeping.co.uk/content.php?sid=48
89>

"Feeding Your Fish: Diet, Nutrition, How and What Fish
Eat." FishKeeping.co.uk.
<http://www.fishkeeping.co.uk/articles_52/fish-diet.htm>

"Feeding Your Fish." First Tank Guide.
<http://www.firsttankguide.net/food.php>

2.) Care for Ghost Knifefish

Ghost Knifefish can be a tricky species to take care of, especially if you are not used to sensitive species of fish. In this section you will find a number of resources with valuable information regarding the care of Ghost Knifefish.

United States Websites:

"Black Ghost Knifefish." TropicalFishKeeping.com. <http://www.tropicalfishkeeping.com/profiles/black-ghost-knifefish/>

"Black Ghost Knife Fish." Aquarium Advice. <http://www.aquariumadvice.com/forums/f29/black-ghost-knife-fish-profile-by-aidan-261639.html>

"Black Ghost Knifefish." Animal-World. <http://animal-world.com/encyclo/fresh/Knifefish/BlackGhostKnifefish.php>

United Kingdom Websites:

"Adding Knifefish to Your Tropical Fish Tank." Tropical Fish Expert. <http://www.tropicalfishexpert.co.uk/knifefish.html>

"Knifefish." Tropical Fish Finder. <http://www.tropicalfishfinder.co.uk/news_article.asp?id=2274>

"New Aquarium Haunt for Ghost Knifefish." Deep Sea World. <http://www.deepseaworld.com/new-aquarium-haunt-for-ghostly-knifefish>

3.) *Health Info for Ghost Knifefish*

No matter how well you take care of them, your Ghost Knifefish are bound to be exposed to disease at some point during their lives. In this section you will find additional resources regarding aquarium fish diseases and treatments.

United States Websites:

"FAQs on Knifefish Disease." WetWebMedia.com. <http://www.wetwebmedia.com/fwsubwebindex/knifedisfaqs.htm>

"Freshwater Fish Disease Symptoms and Treatment." Fishlore. <http://www.fishlore.com/Disease.htm>

Rao, M. Vishwas. "Diseases in the Aquarium Fishes: Challenges and Areas of Concern." International Journal of Environment. <http://www.nepjol.info/index.php/IJE/article/view/9216>

"Chart for Illness and Treatment." Fishnet.org. <http://www.fishnet.org/sick-fish-chart.htm>

United Kingdom Websites:

"Ich (White Spot)." FishForever.co.uk.
<http://www.fishforever.co.uk/ich.html>

"Fish Treatments." Fish, Tanks and Ponds.
<http://www.fishtanksandponds.co.uk/fish-
health/treatments.html>

"Keep Your Fish Healthy." Think Fish.
<http://www.thinkfish.co.uk/article/keep-your-aquarium-
fish-in-top-health>

"Healthy Aquarium Fish." World of Water.
<http://www.worldofwater.co.uk/pages/Healthy-
Aquarium-Fish.html>

4.) General Info for Ghost Knifefish

The more you know about your Ghost Knifefish, the more equipped you will be to provide them with the best care possible. In this section you will find a number of resources providing general information about Ghost Knifefish.

United States Websites:

"Black Ghost Knifefish – Apteronotus albifrons." Badman's Tropical Fish.
<http://badmanstropicalfish.com/profiles/profile66.html>

Leebelt, Jessica. "Electric Oddball." Aquaria Central.
<http://www.aquariacentral.com/fishinfo/fresh/ bghost.shtml>

"Black Ghost Knifefish." LiveAquaria.com.
<http://www.liveaquaria.com/product/prod_display.cfm?c= 747+870+857&pcatid=857>

"Black Ghost Knife – Apteronotus albifrons." Aquatic Community. <http://www.aquaticcommunity.com/fish/ blackghostknife.php>

United Kingdom Websites:

"Apteronotus albifrons – Black Ghost Knifefish." Fish, Tanks and Ponds. <http://www.fishtanksandponds.co.uk/profiles/apteronotus-albifrons.html>

"Black Ghost Knifefish." Live Aquatics. <http://www.liveaquatics.co.uk/shop/knifefish/black-ghost-knife/367>

"Black Ghost Knifefish." Think Fish. <http://www.thinkfish.co.uk/fish/black-ghost-knifefish.html>

Index

A

B

C

D

E

F

G

H

I

J

K

L

Q

R

S

T

Photo Credits

Front Cover Page Photo By RateMyFishTank user Sk8terguy1206, http://www.ratemyfishtank.com/photo-main.php/7973

Back Cover Page Photo By Manage your freshwater aquarium, http://freshwater-aquarium-passion.blogspot.com.au/2010/08/black-ghost knifefish_05.html

Page 1 Photo By RateMyFishTank user Fishnoob17, <http://www.ratemyfishtank.com/photo-main.php/9267>

Page 6 Photo By Derek Ramsey via Wikimedia Commons, <http://en.wikipedia.org/wiki/File:Black_Ghost_Knifefish_4 00.jpg>

Page 7 Photo Orthosternarchus_tamandua, By Boulenger G.A. via Wikimedia Commons, <http://en.wikipedia.org/wiki/File:Orthosternarchus_taman dua.png>

Page 13 Photo Fish Evolution By Epipelagic via Wikimedia Commons, <http://en.wikipedia.org/wiki/File:Fish_evolution.png>

Page 17 Photo Aba Knifefish By Ken Childs via Animal-World.com, <http://animal-world.com/encyclo/fresh/Knifefish/AbaKnifefish.php>

Page 18 Photo African Knifefish By Wiki-Harfus via Wikimedia Commons, <http://en.wikipedia.org/wiki/File:Gymnarchus_niloticus005.JPG>

Page 19 Photo Centipede Knifefish By Ken Childs via Animal-World.com, <http://animal-world.com/encyclo/fresh/Knifefish/CentipedeKnifefish.php

Page 20 Photo Glass Knifefish By Ken Childs via Animal-World.com, <http://animal-world.com/encyclo/fresh/Knifefish/GlassKnifefish.php>

Page 21 Photo Clown Knifefish By Mistvan via Wikimedia Commons, <http://en.wikipedia.org/wiki/File:Chitala.chitala-ZOO.Brno.jpg>

Page 22 Photo Zebra Knifefish By Ken Childs via Animal-World.com, <http://animal-world.com/encyclo/fresh/Knifefish/ZebraKnifefish.php>

Page 23 Photo Reticulate Knifefish By Ken Childs via Animal-World.com, <http://animal-world.com/encyclo/fresh/Knifefish/ReticulateKnifefish.php

Page 24 Photo Black Ghost By Ken Childs via Animal-World.com, <http://animal-world.com/encyclo/fresh/Knifefish/BlackGhostKnifefish.php>

Page 27 Photo By RateMyFishTank user Jomuz, <http://www.ratemyfishtank.com/photo-main.php/11293>

Page 31 Photo By RateMyFishTank user Fishnoob17, <http://www.ratemyfishtank.com/photo-main.php/9272>

Page 40 Photo By RateMyFishTank user Fishnoob17,
<http://www.ratemyfishtank.com/photo-main.php/9268>

Page 46 Photo By RateMyFishTank user PEJMAN84,
<http://www.ratemyfishtank.com/photo-main.php/14638>

Page 48 Photo purchased from Dreamstime

Page 51 Photo Nitrogen Cycle By Eliashc via Wikimedia
Commons, <http://en.wikipedia.org/wiki/
File:Aquarium_Nitrogen_Cycle.png>

Page 54 Photo purchased from Dreamstime

Page 57 Photo purchased from Dreamstime

Page 67 Photo By RateMyFishTank user Mzdanows,
<http://www.ratemyfishtank.com/photo-main.php/17851>

Page 74 Photo By RateMyFishTank user Jia_J,
<http://www.ratemyfishtank.com/photo-main.php/32119>

Page 92 Photo By RateMyFishTank user Baby_Gonzales, <http://www.ratemyfishtank.com/photo-main.php/38446>

References

"A How To on Breeding Black Ghost Knife Fish." FishForums.com. <http://www.fishforums.com/forum/breeding-freshwater-fish/19029-how-breeding-black-ghost-knife-fish.html>

"Aquarium Filter Selection Guide." Drs. Foster and Smith. <http://www.drsfostersmith.com/pic/article.cfm?articleid=304>

"Black Ghost Knifefish." Aquarium Industries. <http://www.aquariumindustries.com.au/wp-content/uploads/2012/07/Ghost-Knife-Fish.pdf>

"Check List of the Freshwater Fishes of South and Central America." The Central Library Pontificia Universidade Catolica de Rio Grande do Sul. Copyright 2003 Edipuers. <http://books.google.com/books?id=9tiDHrzxf9QC&pg=PA497&lpg=PA497&dq=apteronotids&source=bl&ots=m7GZyXVmSI&sig=35gIYiuwoidgP-RZJNtMPenOnYI&hl=en&sa=X&ei=jAFMU_W8FKessQSdj4GABA&ved=0CDMQ6AEwAQ#v=onepage&q&f=false>

"Determining the Sex of Ghost Knifefish." Monster Fishkeepers. <http://www.monsterfishkeepers.com/forums/showthread.php?139894-Determining-the-sex-of-a-black-ghost-knife>

"Fish Treatments." Fish, Tanks and Ponds. <http://www.fishtanksandponds.co.uk/fish-health/treatments.html>

"Freshwater Fish Disease Symptoms and Treatment." Fishlore. <http://www.fishlore.com/Disease.htm>

Glass, Spencer. "Knifefish Knowledge." FishChannel.com. <http://www.fishchannel.com/freshwater-aquariums/species-info/knifefish/knifefish-knowledge.aspx>

"Glossary of Aquarium Terms. Sea and Sky. <http://www.seasky.org/aquarium/aquarium-glossary.html>

"How to Choose Healthy Fish: Avoiding Sick Fish in Your Tank." SetupTank.com. <http://www.setuptank.com/2012/07/how-to-choose-healthy-fish-avoid-sick-fish/>

"Importing and Exporting Live Fish, Mollusks and Crustacea." Gov.uk. < https://www.gov.uk/importing-and-exporting-live-fish-molluscs-and-crustacea>

Kagle, Rebecca. "The Evolutionary Steps of Fish." Serendip Studio. <http://serendip.brynmawr.edu/exchange/node/1904>

"Knifefish." Animal-World.com. <http://animal-world.com/encyclo/fresh/Knifefish/Knifefish.php>
"Three Classes of Fish." The Remarkable Ocean World – CourseWorld.com. <http://www.courseworld.com/ocean/fishes.html>

"Lighting Guide." Drs. Foster and Smith. <http://www.drsfostersmith.com/pic/article.cfm?articleid=414>

Monks, Neale. "Aquarium Fish Finrot." FishChannel.com. <http://www.fishchannel.com/fish-health/disease-prevention/finrot.aspx>

Monks, Neale. "Freshwater Velvet Disease." FishChannel.com. <http://www.fishchannel.com/fish-health/freshwater-conditions/velvet-disease.aspx>

"Nocturnal Lights Simulate Moonlight." Drs. Foster and Smith. <http://www.drsfostersmith.com/pic/article.cfm?aid=553>

Back Cover Text

Ghost Knifefish are unique and beautiful creatures that can make stunning additions to the home aquarium. In order to take good care of your new pet you need to learn everything you can about them. Here you will find information about buying and raising Ghost Knifefish as well as tips for housing, feeding and breeding them.

In this book you will find the answers to all of your questions about Ghost Knifefish – even those you didn't know you had! By the end of this book you will be equipped with all the knowledge you need to give your Ghost Knifefish the best care you can.

CPSIA information can be obtained
at www.ICGtesting.com
Printed in the USA
LVOW02s0502210717
542108LV00011B/137/P